Effective Writing For Feds

By Donald G. Rider

COMMUNICATIONS

FPMI Communications, Inc.

707 Fiber Street

Huntsville, Alabama 35801

(205) 539-1850

Fax (205) 539-0911

Printed in July 1992

ISBN 0-936295-25-2

This book is dedicated to Ray and Harriet, teachers of style and substance.

Table of Contents

Introduction

Effective Writing For Feds

Introduction

While this was not an easy book to write, my students helped. In teaching writing workshops over the years, I've encountered hundreds of students. Their backgrounds and abilities were diverse but they all shared one thing in common; each of them wanted to write more effectively. If you find the rules and concepts outlined in this book to be helpful, substantial credit goes my students. In trying to communicate what is good and bad about someone else's writing, you become a much harsher critic of your own prose.

I quickly encountered two major hurdles in trying to give advice about good writing. The first is the subjective nature of a person's writing style. What may appear as short, crisp or economical writing to one person, seems spare or skeletal to another. ("You need to flesh it out.") The recent trend in both government and legal writing has been to use simpler words and phrases and to do away with all the "attached hereto's" and "promulgated hereunders." Many of my students tell me the simpler, more understandable forms sound better but their superiors won't accept them. "It doesn't sound educated enough" say some reviewers. "We want to sound smart" says another. So our letters to agency clients have to say "termination date" instead of "due date." We must take an action under the "purview" of a rule or regulation. Heaven forbid, we should merely act under a rule or regulation.

The second major hurdle I encountered is the vast number of choices placed before us. It's tough to decide what to include in a writing book and what to leave out. If you've visited a restaurant with too many choices on the menu, you know exactly what I mean. Effective writing certainly requires proper spelling, punctuation and grammar. The right words must be capitalized. If the noun we use in sentences is plural, it just doesn't roll off the tongue unless we link it up with the plural form of the verb (contractors were competing, not contractors was competing).

If spelling, grammar and punctuation are one ingredient of the stew that is effective writing, then sound word choices, action verbs and tight sentences are the meat and potatoes. Like a hearty stew, this book has blended key ingredients but left out some optional items. We have left it to others to address the basics of English grammar and composition. Likewise, focusing on the correct "format" for a letter or memorandum would be of little help since government agencies have such radical variations. Instead, our concentration is on those style issues that deliver the most bang for the buck. By distilling sound writing into these few pages, we've admittedly left out some things.

What have we kept? We've tried to retain the rules, tips and techniques that you can put to work first thing tomorrow morning when you arrive at work. In each chapter, our goal is to deliver immediately useful information—to make the largest impact upon your writing skills with the least pain and suffering for the reader. We've kept it simple for two reasons. First, as a busy government professional, you don't have the time or the inclination to memorize a complete set of writing rules. Second, you've got a lot to think about already. We have kept the rules few and the key points as readable as possible.

Notice also that the chapters in this book are short and that each chapter concludes with writing exercises. Once again, the reasoning is simple and based upon the experiences of my writing students. Neither you nor I can learn about writing by simply reading someone's hints, tips, or writing rules. You have to do it. Writing must be practiced. For this reason, each chapter gives you an opportunity to apply the key points about effective writing which have been discussed.

Chapter One

Different Writing Styles For Different Purposes

CHAPTER 1

Different Writing Styles For Different Purposes

Each of us has developed our own very special, very personal writing style. Sometimes, you can even recognize a person by his writing style. This is often true of your co-workers or your supervisor. The way people write is distinctive. Even if the document is unsigned, you often know after the first couple of sentences, "that's Jeanette's writing," or "that's Phil's writing."

You may work in an office where the boss favors "cookie cutter" writing. He wants all letters or memoranda produced by the work unit to sound the same. This is especially so if several staffers are producing drafts, but the final product is going out over the supervisor's signature. I cannot reform your boss or loosen the reigns, unleashing your creative juices. What this chapter can do is help you isolate the key components of your own writing style. In this way, the task of producing acceptable drafts becomes easier.

Each of us has more than one trademark writing style. Consciously or subconsciously, we adapt sentence structure, word choices—even the pace of our writing, depending upon what we want to accomplish. The underlying purpose of a given document controls the way we should approach a writing assignment. It is too easy to get sidetracked concerning the type of document (memorandum, letter, briefing paper, appeal) and lose sight of the document's objective. The techniques we are going to examine will apply no matter what the title of your document.

Let's begin by focusing on who you are writing for and why the document is being created. It is only after we have jumped this first critical hurdle, that we can begin to think about crafting sound sentences and paragraphs.

What Are The Major Writing Styles And When Do I Use Them?

Description

This writing style aims to make the reader hear, smell, taste or feel the subject matter. It tries to elevate the reader's interest level so that she is drawn to the subject of the document. Individual word choices, as well as the the order in which the words hang together in the sentence, take on tremendous importance.

Catchy advertising is one of the best examples of descriptive writing. Word choices are selected to create a mental image for the potential buyer. After digesting the best real estate copy, you can almost smell the bread baking in the oven.

> Two years young Cape Cod in desirable family neighborhood. Set high on a hill with incomparable view of city. This home is decorated in earth-tones and is in pristine condition. Walk to award-winning schools and shopping.

Sports journalism also follows the descriptive writing style. After all, the sports columnist is trying to recreate the sights, sounds, smells and emotion of field action through written images.

> Higgins' touchdown ramble highlighted a 17 point quarter for the Red Devils, whose explosive offense had been completely shut down until that point. The point after attempt was squashed by the extra human effort of Ted Hendricks who made an airborne lunge through the gap.

Of what help is all this "hype" to the government writer? After all, we're not sending out advertising copy or covering sporting events. While that's true, we are often trying to paint a vivid picture of abstract events. In seeking a budget increase for one of our field offices, a little descriptive writing may help bring the problem home. Consider excerpts from pleas for a budget increase; the first drafted in a plodding style, full of stale terms; the second strengthened by descriptive writing.

Version A

The Hanover field office has struggled all year to provide adequate client services. Insufficient staffing levels and high turnover have resulted in the slowest case processing time in the Region. Only a 15% increase in Title XVI funds will alleviate this problem.

Version B

Hanover has become the poor stepchild among Region III's field offices. Last year, five capable claims representatives attacked the case backlog, only to lose heart and seek reassignments. Exit interviews revealed these comments: "The office space was cold, dingy and depressing;" "We were fighting a losing battle every day."

Narration

In narrative writing, our focus is upon placing important details in the proper order. The centerpiece of our writing is how the incidents or events fit together. We want to tell a coherent and understandable story which is easy to follow. Compare this to descriptive writing. In a description, the central aim is to place the reader in the setting, atmosphere or mood. We want to leave the reader with a gut level feel for the emotion of the event. In narration, our purpose is different. The proper focus is upon the order, sequence or flow of events.

Many of the written products churned out by government professionals fall into this category. In writing an investigative report or merely compiling minutes of a meeting, we are engaged in narrative writing. Perhaps you have attended a conference, training session or meeting and your boss has asked for a recap of what took place. This assignment clearly calls for narration.

Effective fiction writers use narration in much the same way a good government writer does. The fiction writer wants to place the reader in the correct time and place to help him get his bearings. Often, when you start a novel and then put it down unfinished, it's because you are exasperated with the author's poor narration. How can you enjoy the story when you can't easily track what is happening? Notice how clear, simple narrative sentences not only tell a story, but also form the events into a logical sequence.

> It was just before the start of the fall semester. The oaks and birches along the canyon wall recorded only a hint of autumn color. This would be Rita's last caving adventure before she turned her attention to books, papers and exams, on September 4.

Notice how this preliminary paragraph places us in time. We are obviously in the late summer and are dealing with a college student who enjoys exploring caves. Our narration has even created the suspicion that some coming event may interrupt the normal start of Rita's school semester. The paragraph would no doubt be followed by subsequent paragraphs describing what happened on the caving trip.

As government writers, we are constantly called upon to convey events and details in a logical order. In one agency where I worked, senior managers were considering discipline against a high ranking official based upon an unauthorized speech he made. The managers asked the Human Resources staff for background information on the employee. What they received was a piece of strong narrative writing.

> Todd Pantera delivered a speech to the "Budgeting for Local Government" Workshop on August 5 in Atlanta. During the speech he took positions on budgeting procedures which were in direct conflict with the Department's policies. On two occasions just prior to leaving for the workshop, his supervisor directed Pantera to supply him with a copy of the upcoming speech. Pantera did not comply with these requests.

The writer has indeed told a story, but has not stuck to strict chronological order. We are told about the second event first—the speech itself. Then the writer moves backwards in time to an earlier occurrence—the refusal to provide a draft or advance copy of the speech. Is this poor organization? Is this accidental? Probably not. We are told of the more important event first (the actual delivery of the speech). The narrative then moves back in time to cover the events leading up to the speech.

This writing technique, known as "inversion," is used to add variety to writing and help hold the reader's attention.

Exposition

Exposition is detailed writing. Its focus is on explanation. The writer may be trying to explain a situation, a process, a viewpoint or simply tell us why a carefully planned meeting turned out to be a disaster. When using this style it is important to sound unbiased.

Exposition conveys the idea that the writer is a competent, careful and deliberate individual with no axe to grind. She is trying to convince the reader that a complete picture is at hand. No important stone has been left unturned; no detail ignored. A specialized group of writers called "technical writers" are the masters of exposition. If you have purchased a new appliance recently, the owner's manual was authored by a technical writer. His task is not to persuade, entertain or enliven. His focus is upon the facts and he pays meticulous attention to detail. Clarity, detail and simplicity are the hallmarks of the expository writer.

The manager of a government motor pool was called to task because her mechanics had a very slow turn around time in completing repair orders. See for yourself how her response follows this approach:

During the past two fiscal years, the average time required to service, repair and return vehicles to their drivers has increased from .9 days to 1.5 days. This "downtime" rate is wholly unacceptable to me. There are four specific reasons for this rate increase:

1. The addition last year of engine overhauls to our previous responsibilities involving only routine maintenance;

2. A 10% budget cut and a corresponding decrease in our in-stock parts inventory;

3. The permanent loss of one mechanic and one mechanic helper position;

4. An increase in the size and composition of our fleet leading to more frequent and complex repair orders.

Legal Writing

The purpose of legal writing is to persuade. Briefs, legal memoranda and appeals are all aimed at bringing the reader around to your point of view. Legal writing tries to move people, to induce them to "buy off" on your own position or viewpoint. Much legal writing suffers from stuffiness, complexity and the use of ancient Latin terms. It is often so boring to read that it's a home cure for insomnia.

Occasionally, a piece of legal writing provides pleasant reading. It's light and airy or even humorous. Somehow, it just "flows." But this is a side show—a fringe benefit. If a legal document informs, explains, enlightens or entertains the well drafted document does so in support of its overall mission—persuasion. These additional features only supplement or enhance the writer's main thrust which is to bring you around to her point of view.

The analytical approach demanded by legal writing is illustrated by the "IRAC" system. This straightforward system suggests that sound legal documents should be organized around four basic concepts—Issue, Rule, Analysis and Conclusion (IRAC). But first, a few definitions will be helpful.

> ***Issue:*** *The central question or controversy to be decided.*

Example:

> ***Issue:*** Did Sue Cook violate agency ethics regulations when she accepted free tuition to a professional conference on the latest trends in government procurement?

> ***Rule:*** *The policy, rule, principle, regulation, law or case which should be applied to resolve a given issue.*

Example:

A) Ethics Rule 2.1 prohibits the acceptance of any gratuity by a government employee from an organization seeking to do business with the government;

B) Ethics Rule 2.2 permits a waiver of course or conference tuition for government employees making bona fide presentations at a professional symposium.

Analysis: The process of applying a rule to a given set of facts.

Sue Cook's actions involved acceptance of a gratuity. The course tuition had a dollar value of $325 and the conference sponsor was an organization seeking to do business with her agency (or) Sue Cook acted within the bounds of agency ethics regulations since she presented a one hour workshop on bid solicitations in return for her tuition waiver.

Conclusion: The bottom line, outcome, or course of action compelled by your analysis.

Sue Cook violated ethics regulations and is therefore subject to discipline (or) Sue Cook acted within the bounds of agency ethics regulations and no action against her is warranted.

The "IRAC" Writing System

- State the Issue
- State the rule or policy to be applied.
- Analyze by applying the rule to a set of facts
- Conclusion compelled by your analysis

An illustration will help explain each of the four key components of the IRAC method. This is how two legal writers arguing different sides of a case might use "IRAC" in organizing their document:

Question: Should Robert Duvall be suspended from work for 30 days for pushing his supervisor during an argument?

Version A (Written by a manager supporting the 30 days suspension)

> At 2 p.m. on March 13, Robert Duvall confronted his supervisor, picked a fight with him and pushed him to the ground bruising his shoulder. Agency regulation 711.23 clearly outlaws this conduct. The table of penalties states that pushing, shoving or striking a supervisor warrants at least a 15 day suspension up to and including termination of the offending employee. Physical assault of a supervisor is inexcusable. To tolerate this kind of gross misconduct would destroy workplace discipline. Therefore, the 30 day suspension is completely justified and should not be disturbed by the reviewing official.

Version B (Written by the Employee's Representative attempting to overturn the suspension)

> On March 13, Branch Chief John Steadman hurled a series of insults at one of his employees. Only after this blatant provocation and in self-defense, did Bob Duvall gently push Steadman away. According to Robert Bray, a noted authority on discipline, "severe discipline is not appropriate where an employee is provoked or harassed by his supervisor and then retaliates. Bray, *Discipline at Work*, (Simon and Schuster, New York, 1989) p. 107.

How have each of the writers applied IRAC in this case? Both writers are dealing with precisely the same issue which turns upon the appropriateness of the discipline. But interestingly, each has applied a different rule. Each writer has referred to a rule or authority which best supports his position. The manager arguing in favor of the suspension has cited an agency regulation prohibiting physical contact with a supervisor as well as the existing table of penalties. The employee representative would prefer to focus elsewhere. He has relied on an expert opinion, bringing to bear the viewpoint of an outsider. How can a 30 day suspension be proper, where an employee is simply responding to abuse and standing up for himself?

Next, each writer turns to analysis, the second part of the IRAC scheme. Our management writer reasons that physical assault of a supervisor justifies very severe discipline. To ignore these actions, or to show lenience, would send the wrong message to everyone else at work.

The employee representative views things differently. There are special circumstances here—provocation. No severe discipline is appropriate since the incident would never have taken place had it not been for the supervisor's actions.

Finally, let's examine each writer's conclusion. Our management author minces no words. "[T]he 15 day suspension..should not be disturbed." Our employee proponent reaches a very different conclusion: "Severe discipline is not appropriate."

EXERCISES

1. Rewrite the following passages, making them more descriptive.

A. When Sue arrived at work it was still dark outside. She went into her office and turned on her computer. Only at this point did she look across her partition to see co-worker John slumped over his desk.

B. You will find Federal employment both exciting and challenging. There is ample opportunity for career development. Training is provided, and the pay and benefits are excellent.

2. Develop a paragraph which places the following events in a logical narrative form. Rewrite as necessary.

A. In fact, the storm caused many roads to become impassable.

B. On November 11 employees were told that absences the previous day would be excused.

C. The following day a severe snowstorm did hit the area, paralyzing traffic.

D. On the evening of November 9, Channel 7 predicted a substantial snowfall.

E. Many employees could not get into work on November 10.

3. Use exposition to pack more detail into these sentences.

A. Government employees can't accept gifts from certain contractors.

B. You will receive a step pay increase next year unless you are already at the top step.

4. Use exposition to remove the biased viewpoint from these sentences. Give each sentence a neutral viewpoint .

A. Our manpower needs for next fiscal year will only be met if we can extort more money from the Cabinet Secretary.

B. It is a waste of our time and resources for agency employees to speak before bleeding-heart environmental groups. These groups are lying in wait to attack each and every position we take.

5. Using the facts below, write a one paragraph memorandum to Sara Covington recommending that Lofgren receive a written reprimand. Write a second paragraph arguing against any discipline. (Hint: the IRAC method may help you better organize your paragraph.)

Facts

Bob Lofgren blew a major deadline last week causing his agency to lose a potential $50,000 in matching federal funds for a storm sewer upgrade. The Section Manager, Sara Covington, is considering issuing Lofgren a letter or reprimand. There are two rules which may apply to this situation. The first is that irresponsibility or neglect of duties causing economic hardship to the agency, is cause for discipline. A second rule states that management may elect not to discipline an employee where the infraction was due to unusual personal circumstances, and is not likely to reoccur.

Chapter Two

Making Sentences and Paragraphs Work For You

Chapter 2

Making Sentences And Paragraphs Work For You

Sentences and paragraphs are basic tools of the writer just as the hammer and saw are basic to the cabinet maker's trade. Sentences and paragraphs are the raw material we use to craft words into a final written product. As we've seen in the previous chapter, our final product may inform, explain, illustrate or even persuade. At its best, good writing even provides some pleasure to the audience. There are some basic rules about constructing sentences which will help you deliver a better product to your reader.

Use A Spoken Style And Focus On The Reader

Readers hear writing. Therefore, the most easily understood writing sounds like people talking. You may even find it helpful to imagine your reader sitting across the room from you while you compose a draft. Try reading it aloud. Does it sound like something you might say to a person?

One way in which we draw the reader in, is to make our prose reader-centered. When you are conversing with someone, she is quickly turned off by a conversation that focuses only on the speaker's needs, concerns, or accomplishments ("self-centered"). After a few minutes of *I, I, I,* the speaker's orientation becomes irritating. The same thing is true in written communication. For this reason, focus your sentences on the reader's concerns—not your concerns as the writer.

Writer-Centered	Reader-Oriented
The service we provide must meet our client's needs.	The service you receive must be top flight.
We are closed every evening except Wednesday, when we remain open until 9 p.m.	For your convenience, we are open until 9 p.m. each Wednesday.
I would like to express my appreciation for your first rate job. Your report helped us meet a critical deadline.	Thank you for a first rate job.

Focus your writing on the readers' concerns rather than your interests as the writer. This makes your writing more interesting and more effective.

Put Sentences In The Affirmative, Rather Than The Negative Mode

As readers, we understand affirmative sentences more easily than we do negative ones. Affirmative sentences register more quickly, avoid a mental struggle, and are processed more efficiently by the brain. Listen for negative writing and try to avoid it unless you have some special reason to caution the reader.

Negative Mode	Positive Mode
Breaks may not begin until 9:30 a.m.	Breaks may be taken anytime after 9:30 a.m.
Our comments on the proposed rule will not be available until November 13.	The comments on the proposed rule will be available on November 13.
Opportunities for promotion are severely limited.	Competition for these positions is particularly keen.

Keep the Subject and the Verb Close Together

To make your writing easy to understand, most of your sentences should follow a traditional word order. The subject of a sentence is stated and it is followed in short order by the verb. When you leave a large gap between the subject of your sentence and the verb, you are asking too much of the reader. You are asking her to be a reading athlete; to make a huge leap while still keeping straight in her mind what you are talking about.

> A procurement request, which must be filled out in triplicate, and in the case of sole source purchases must contain a detailed supporting statement, is filed with the contracting office.

In this example, the subject of the sentence is "Procurement request" and the verb is "filed." In the sentence above the reader must leap twenty-two words from the subject to the verb. By the time she reaches the end of the sentence, she may have forgotten its purpose The simplest remedy for this writing disease is to divide the overall thought into several shorter sentences.

> Procurement requests are to be filed with the contracting office. They are to be submitted in triplicate. If the purchase is from a sole source vendor, the request must contain a detailed supporting statement.

Experiment With Mini-Sentences

Occasional sentences of six words or less focus the reader's attention, provide variety, and add emphasis. Try some. Be cautious not to use this technique so often that it becomes a writing mannerism or gimmick.

> We could overlook these unplanned absences if they were occasional. They aren't. You have requested emergency leave nine times in the last six pay periods.

> Our branch felt that it could weather the latest budget crisis without RIF's. It cannot. Immediate measures will have to be taken to pare our personnel costs.

Locate Ideas Deliberately Within A Sentence To Emphasize Or Down Play Them

A writer does with ink on paper what a speaker does with voice inflection, gestures and bearing. The writer is denied a speaker's advantages so he must craft his sentences carefully, always searching for maximum effect. Begin and end a sentence any way you prefer. Keep in mind however, that ideas which are are placed at the beginning or end of a sentence gain emphasis.

If you wish to mute or downplay an idea, place it in the middle of the sentence.

Examples

I want to take this opportunity to thank you for a job well done. (This emphasizes "job well done.")

You did a great job on this project and I want to thank you for your fine effort (emphasizes "you.).

We will want to recognize and reward other strong performers, if this overall level of effort continues (mutes "other strong performers").

Effective Paragraphs

Fast Start / Slow Start

Readers expect a paragraph to have a central theme or topic. They also anticipate that the first sentence of a paragraph will state the topic. If we look for this "lead-in" or "topic sentence" format as readers, then why are we so stingy in using it as writers? Perhaps because we paragraph from the gut. We instinctively end one paragraph and begin another where we **feel** a natural breaking point.

Readers need to know your main point early so they can appreciate the relevance of whatever else you say. If you delay, they must read your writing twice—once to see where the details are headed and again to understand the details in perspective. To help the reader, open with your main point, much the way newspaper articles do. ("A devastating hurricane struck the Gulf Coast of Florida this morning.")

While it may be appropriate for a mystery writer to feed us one clue at a time, conventional writers should tell us immediately the direction in which we are headed. Jump right in! Instead of building up to the main point, put it in the first paragraph.

As with sentences, the points you wish to emphasize should be placed at the very beginning of the paragraph, or at the very end, since these are areas the reader will focus upon. When you are delivering bad news, or want to soften an idea, place it in the middle of a paragraph.

In the following paragraph, the writer had an important message but buried it in the middle, where it will not receive the attention it deserves:

Slow Start

> Several new building security measures will take effect on April 1. Access to the building will no longer be available through the rear loading dock. Both the fitness center and the computer room will be outfitted with electronic locks and access to these areas will be limited to those possessing the correct computer-coded ID card. In addition, all automobiles entering or exiting the employee parking lot will be subject to physical search as will vehicle occupants. We have implemented these new procedures in response to a series of recent thefts in the building and the need to secure valuable agency property.

Fast Start

Effective April 1, both vehicles and vehicle occupants entering our parking lot will be subject to physical search. This measure was required because of the unprecedented thefts of agency computer and electronic equipment over the past several months. Several other changes in security procedures will take place on the same date. The computer room and fitness center may only be accessed by computer-coded cards. Building access will be restricted to the main entrance on 33rd Street.

Linking Paragraphs With Smooth Transitions

Paragraphs are usually linked by transitions. To insure a smooth flow between two paragraphs, we want either:

- The first paragraph to lead into the second, or;

- The second to refer back to the first. As a writer, this bridge between paragraphs is filled with potholes.

We guarantee failure when we insist on stale overused bridges ("The next factor to consider is....")

Transitional words must be used with precision. Common bridge words like "yet" and "however" are often used incorrectly. Each word signals a change in direction, much as does the phrase "on the other hand." Effective writers vary their bridges. You don't want to use "however" or "therefore" five times in a row. Readers become irritated by this. Try some of the following in closing out your paragraph or starting off a new one. Each of these transitions can be effective if used in the right spot.

Introducing a New Thought or Idea

In general
In the first place
To begin with

Wrapping Up a Thought or Closely Linked Set of Events

To conclude
To sum up
To summarize
Finally
As we have seen
As a result
In short

Recapping or Restating

That is
In other words
To be sure
In particular

Emphasize Key Point, Fact or Event

To be sure
In effect
Above all
Not only...but also

Draw a Comparison or Contrast

In contrast	Actually
Although	Nevertheless
Despite	

Keeping Times, Places and Events in Sequence

Afterwards	Eventually
Later	Ultimately
Initially	This time
From the very beginning	The Next Time

Use Short Paragraphs for Spice, Variety and Emphasis

A short sentence lends emphasis to a key point. A short paragraph does the same. It is used for special effect. It can highlight a major transition, emphasize an important conclusion or summarize a grouping of paragraphs. Long paragraphs swamp important ideas. When you add white space to a document you increase the ease of reading.

A single sentence paragraph helps highlight a special idea.

EXERCISES

1. Revise the following passages to make them more reader-centered.

> We are building a reputation for quality service and eliminating errors. When we deliver better client service, everyone benefits.
>
> I cannot release the documents until 1 p.m. on Friday, October 18. Photocopies will be provided only if you make a specific request for them.

2. Revise these sentences so that the subject and the verb are closer together. If necessary, divide the thoughts into two separate sentences.

> Recommendations for cash awards, which must be endorsed by both the Section Chief and the Division Manager, must be received by December 1.
>
> Whether ordering office supplies, or purchasing new office equipment, keep in mind standards for SF-23, a copy of which is attached.

3. Develop and insert transition sentences in the blank spaces.

(A)

The cooperative education program has produced a handful of good job candidates for us but has not been cost-effective. Our expenses have simply outstripped the yield of qualified new workers.

One alternative would be increased participation in job fairs. Perhaps we could offer cash bonuses to current agency employees who bring us qualified applicants. Some agencies have had success with upward mobility candidates from within the organization.

(B)

In my opinion the training conference was unfocused and poorly organized. Sessions did not start on time and my speaker seemed ill-prepared. Some speakers rambled and did not cover the advertised topics.

Among the possibilities for improving this annual event would be to hire a professional conference planner or to appoint a committee of key employees to oversee its execution.

Chapter Three

Simplify, Simplify, Simplify

Chapter 3

Simplify, Simplify, Simplify

"Pompous words are the signs of egomaniacs trying to show off their education, power or vocabulary"

Anonymous

Bad writing is full of excess baggage. Not only are the sentences too long, but the words lack precision. Poor writers often use clusters of four or five words where two or three will do the job more effectively. Many of us know we should simplify, but large egos and insecure managers sometimes stand in the way of top notch writing. If you want to show off your power, education or vocabulary, by all means choose the complex over the simple; the lengthy over the short. Review these common word clusters and some straightforward alternatives:

effectuate	begin, carry out
in the majority of instances	usually
enclosed herewith	enclosed
make itself felt	influenced
in the event of	if
as of this date	yet, now
for the purpose of	to
concerning the matter of	about
at this time	now
a number of	several

due to the fact that	because
in accordance with	under
on a quarterly basis	quarterly
subsequent to	after
prior to	before

In my writing workshops, students often resist the idea of substituting simple words for more complicated word clusters. "My supervisor won't approve that," they say. "It doesn't sound educated enough," say others. Throw in a fancy word once in awhile, I tell them. Just stick to simple word choices most of the time. Both you and your supervisor will like the result.

Because readers hear writing much as they hear spoken conversation, the most readable writing sounds like people talking. You are not odd if you read your drafts aloud. Your writing should sound like something you would say to another person. To help you move closer to a spoken style, practice economy. There are some easy methods to help you promote an economical style in your own written drafts.

Maximize Essential Words, Minimize Connectors

Early in my government career, I turned in a draft letter for my supervisor's review. He returned it to me with major changes and written comments such as "too wordy" and "tighten it up." I was not happy about this since I had labored hard on the draft. On the other hand, I knew instinctively that his version of the letter was better than my original. I just wasn't sure why.

This experience made me want to improve. My fragile ego could not withstand a similar hatchet job in the future. I approached my boss and asked how I might "tighten up" my writing. Just what does that mean? How can I cut out all these important words and still get the message across? Talking to my boss was like asking directions from a person who doesn't know street names, route numbers or compass directions (You know, just go down by the 7-11 and turn there by the old fire house across from where Mabel Wilson had the accident last year). He fumbled and stumbled, searching for an explanation I could really use.

We both knew that his version of the letter sounded tighter and more economical than mine, but neither of us could isolate any set of rules, guidelines or benchmarks I could follow in my quest for stronger writing. In the intervening years I did improve my writing and tried to share what I'd learned with others. It turns out that a tighter, more economical writing style is available to anyone with a little patience. You begin by sitting down and thoughtfully examining a piece of your own writing. The good news is that there are some simple diagnostic devices with which to evaluate symptoms, come up with a diagnosis and initiate a cure.

The key is to begin by labeling each of your words as either a brick word (BW) or a mortar word (MW). Simply stated, brick words are those essential to your message; mortar words are not. Mortar words are the glue that hold your sentences and paragraphs together (and, by, but, then, if, so, they, it). On the other hand, brick words are central to the meaning of your written message (sell, buy, cancel, bid, dismiss, untimely, claim, appeal, ignore, grant).

Your writing will take on a smoother flow, become tighter and more persuasive by focusing on brick words and trimming as many mortar words (the fat) as possible. Here is an illustration of the brick vs. mortar concept.

> A review of the bidder's technical qualifications was requested by Axiom Corporation.

With the brick words in bold, the sentence looks something like this:

> A **review** of the **bidders' technical qualification** was **requested** by the **Axiom Corporation.**

The remaining words in the sentence are mortar, or connecting words. These six mortar words do not add to the critical meaning of the sentence; they just help hold it together. Can this sentence be rewritten, making it tighter and reducing the number of mortar words? A revised version might read:

> Axion Corporation requested a review of the bidder's technical qualifications.

In the revised version there are seven brick words, but only three mortar words, a reduction of 50%

from the first draft. The sentence has not changed in meaning. It's simply shorter, tighter and more readable. Let's take a look at a longer sentence:

> The response that was given by Social Services went to the heart of the issue, which was scarce resources.

Emphasizing the brick words, the sentence looks like this:

> The **response** that was **given** by **Social Services** went to the **heart** of the **issue,** which was **scarce resources.**

A quick scan of this sentence reveals nine brick words and eleven mortar words. Now let's try a rewrite, reducing the connecting or mortar words:

> Social Services' response, which went to the heart of the matter, focused upon scarce resources.

The latter version contains eight brick words and only seven mortar words, a reduction in mortar words of some 30%.

Restrict Each Sentence to a Single Thought

Before you put pen to paper, it is important to analyze the audience you are writing for. You will need to adopt or tailor your writing style, depending upon the identity of the reader. No matter your reader's knowledge or education level, the message will be quickly lost in a long, complex sentence. Short, simple sentences can be a powerful tool. The critical questions are these:

- What do I want to accomplish in this written message?
- Who is likely to read it?
- What is the reader's current level of knowledge and sophistication?
- What framework or approach will make it easier for them to act?

The written messages that follow attempt to explain a potential disciplinary situation to three different readers. Each of the readers has a different level of sophistication and knowledge about disciplinary situations. Of equal importance, each reader has a different *need.*

Audience Is Agency Attorney

> Hobgood's actions were a form of self-help. Leaving the job site was a patent breach of the contract. Unless the doctrine of condonation applies, Hobgood is subject to severe discipline.

Audience Is Agency First Line Supervisor

> Hobgood took matters in his own hands. The moment he disobeyed your direct order to return to work he became an illegal striker. So long as you did not agree to his leaving work, you are entitled to write him up for a disciplinary violation. If in your opinion, counseling will take care of the situation, follow that course. The final decision is yours.

Audience Is Pipefitter/Employee

> You left work without permission from your supervisor. In fact, you disobeyed your foreman's direct order to return to the job. You haven't given any reasonable excuse or explanation for what you did. As a result, we are suspending you for five days.

Let's go back and focus on one of the key objectives above. Did we strive to meet our reader's *needs*? We know that every specialty and profession in government service has developed its own technical terms, jargon, and language. This specialty language is a kind of shorthand. We use it to describe processes, events and things that don't always occur outside our field. If written material meets the reader's needs, it will be an aid in decision-making. Have the three readers receiving our disciplinary messages benefited from the messages we sent them?

The Agency Attorney

The attorney is used to dealing with cases, legal principles and competing or conflicting interests. But she doesn't want to read a long rambling message. Our two sentences use three "technical" or legal terms which are important to the attorney:

1. self-help;

2. patent breach; and

3. condonation.

The attorney can quickly focus on these three critical issues, all of which may affect the outcome of this discipline case. Jumping quickly to the computer terminal for research aids, the lawyer can scan cases on condonation and decide whether they will help her evaluate this case. Her research may convince her that the writer has missed the mark completely—the facts have nothing to do with "patent breach." Even this result does not mean total defeat for the writer. You have at least helped the attorney clarify and focus on key issues.

The Supervisor

The supervisor is too busy to be concerned with fancy legal principles. He is paid to get the work done, not to analyze cases. Perhaps at the time this employee problem arose, he was short-staffed because of two people on sick leave and had just learned of a 5% budget cut. What does the supervisor want? What does he need from the writer? The answer is that the supervisor is interested in two things:

options and risks. After all, we pay the manager for judgment and leadership skills, so isn't it logical to give alternatives?

In just four sentences, you have supplied a lot of help. You have clearly communicated,

1. What the employee did;

2. Why the employee was wrong in what he did;

3. Options available to the supervisor in dealing with the situation.

The Employee

The employee's needs and interests as a reader are quite different. The employee is not paid to analyze fact situations or cases. His job duties do not include the oversight and control of the work force. The pipefitter's task is to carry out specific job instructions and to do so promptly and efficiently. Our writer has clearly communicated to the employee precisely what he needs to know to make decisions—what he did wrong and what the consequences will be if he persists in this course of action.

EXERCISES

1. Replace the lengthy word groups with simpler choices.

   A. As of this date, our investigation of the May 23 incident shows that the Branch Chief acted in accordance with established procedures.

   B. This responds to your inquiry concerning the matter of your step increase.

2. Tighten up each passage by maximizing brick words and reducing the number of mortar words.

   A. Often, it is the case that regulations are too poorly written for the taxpayers to understand.

   B. The explanation that was given by Williams did not seem logical.

   C. Accepting gifts or meals from a government contractor is prohibited by ethics regulations in those instances where the employee may play a role in contractor selection.

   D. In the future, there is to be no parking whatsoever in reserved parking spaces, nor in handicapped spaces, unless the employee possesses the appropriate sticker for such spaces.

3. Develop three different versions of the following brief message for each of *three different audiences.*

Message One—To Taxpayers who may file property tax appeals

Message Two—To the Review Staff expected to evaluate and decide the taxpayer appeals

Message Three—To the County Executive who has more than 300 employees working for her, including the property tax review staff.

Facts:

1. Taxpayers who wish to appeal their new property tax assessments must do so by October 1.

2. Tax appeal forms are available by phone (555-1212) or by sending a self-addressed, stamped envelope.

3. Any appeal postmarked after October 1 will not be processed—no exceptions.

4. The review staff will be expected to work overtime throughout October and November.

5. All appeals will be acted upon with 60 days of receipt.

6. The overtime budget is nearly exhausted and the voters are highly irritated with recent increases in property taxes.

Chapter Four

Say What You Mean

Chapter 4

Say What You Mean

"The language must be solemn, make the obvious sound important, soften painful truths, and cause the reader to think that the government is in the hands of profound thinkers whose actions are beyond criticism." Anonymous

Why is it so difficult to say what we mean? In conversation with our friends, we come across loud and clear. They are able to sense precisely what we mean. With written communication it's more difficult. There is no body language attached to a sheet of paper. The writer cannot see our eyes glaze over as he lists his ten favorite quotations from the Code of Federal Regulations. The Procurement Chief on the receiving end of your memo is unable to see your face turn beet red as you remind him for the third time of the new office equipment you ordered four months ago.

Without body language, voice inflection and gestures, the writer must turn to other weapons. At its best, writing can convey urgency, anger and exasperation, humor, respect and awe. All these and more can be found in good writing. But how does the writer do it? How does the skilled mystery novelist send a chill down the reader's spine? How do the best legal writers sound so convincing, so right-thinking, that their logic is unassailable?

It's all done by manipulating words—by selecting the right word choices and then linking them together in a particular order with punctuation in just the right spot. Consider the following message "pairs" which communicate the same underlying thought, but do so in very different ways:

Version A

> The law we enforce guarantees that no American should go hungry. I call on each of you to redouble your efforts in the next two years to make this guarantee a reality.

Version B

> When it passed this law, Congress said that no American should be eating dog food from a can. Your job, during the next budget cycle, is to bring an end to American babies with empty stomachs.

Version A is all right. It's "safe," "neutral" and inoffensive. Version B is far more earthy. The writer paints a picture with words. In Version B, the agency's clients (the hungry) are no longer faceless, no longer anonymous. Most readers have caught a whiff of canned dog food and recall the somewhat offensive odor. The second image, that of a hungry baby, is also familiar to most people. Our writer has made deliberate and conscious decisions about word choices and has used those word choices to maximum effect.

Effective word choices are critical in all facets of government writing. The topic need not be something so dramatic as hunger in America to warrant careful and deliberate word selections.

Consider the following "pairs," lifted from a manager's memo recommending a cash award for one of her employees:

Version A

> Leventhal has not only met all of his performance goals, he has exceeded them. He did a superior job in getting the Title IX regulations out and acted with independence under a minimum of supervision.

Version B

> Leventhal created our Title IX Regulations from scratch. He threw himself into the job of shaping and moulding these new requirements. Leventhal drove himself to ensure that every deadline was met.

Making Conscious Word Choices

Take a few moments to explore the following sets of words. Note that each word in the set is sometimes used as a substitute for the others. But each choice has its own connotation and creates a distinct image in the mind of the reader:

bureaucrat/career civil servant/government worker

intellectual/egghead/scholar

woman/lady/female/gal

cop/policeman/law enforcement officer

work/toil/drudgery

aide/executive assistant/staffer

initiative/new program/mandate

beginning/outset/genesis

Be Selective in Your Level of Formality

In our drive to sound both capable and educated in our writing, we sometimes get carried away. Excess formality in a written document can make writing heavy and stiff. I'm not suggesting that you fill your memos and reports with slang terms. Rather, try to make conscious decisions about the words you select. Keep in mind that there is often both a formal and an informal way to state the same thought. Here is a list of commonly used words with some informal alternatives.

Formal	Informal
afford an opportunity	allow
apprise	inform, tell
cease	stop
commitment	promise
deem	think
demonstrate	show
desire	wish
employ	use
expedite	hasten, hurry
eventuate, transpire	happen
facilitate	ease
implement, effectuate	begin, carry out
locality	place, area
locate	find
prior to	before
render	make, issue
reside	live
subsequent to	after
terminate	end
transmit	send

The Simple vs. The Complex

To give your writing variety, to "mix it up," you will find it helpful to insert a simple word choice from time to time. Your writing will sound stuffy if you consistently select the complex over the simple, the fancy over the plain. Here are some common phrases seen time and again in government writing, along with some straightforward alternatives.

At this time	Now
Due to the fact that	Because
Concerning the matter of	About
In reference to	About
For the purpose of	To
As of this date	Now
In the event of	If
Despite the fact that	Although
In the majority of instances	Usually
On behalf of	For
On the part of	For
Enclosed herewith	Enclosed
Makes itself felt	Influences
Give rise to	Create, originate

Don't Blow the Basics

Have you been to a training conference, seminar or symposium recently? If so, you probably heard some good presentations and some that were not so good. What makes the difference? It's often not the content of the speaker's presentation. He may be a legitimate expert in his area and have invaluable knowledge to share. But suppose he mumbles, speaks in a monotone, or intersperses his talk with "uh, uh" every few seconds. Its distracting isn't it? As a listener, you stop focusing upon the *content* of the speaker's presentation and begin to concentrate upon *annoying distractions.*

Written material is really no different. A sophisticated writer must make the correct word choice and avoid distractions. Not only will you look like an amateur if you blow the basics, but your central message will be lost. Think about the written communications that arrive at your desk each day. If the writer makes a basic error, you tend to discount the rest of what she has written.

The writer pays a high price when using a word out of context. The remainder of the message, which may be critically important, is ignored. You would certainly not submit a memo to your boss containing the phrase "we ain't got no alternatives." The following are common mistakes that can make you look like you're in the minor leagues of writing. Choosing the correct word adds to your professional standing and let's people know that you communicate with authority. The glossary that follows will help you avoid some of the most common mistakes in government writing.

Commonly Misused Terms in Government Writing

Affect/Effect—Effect means to bring about or accomplish a particular result; affect means to influence.

Allege/Allegation—Allege is spelled without a "d." To allege something is to assert it or claim it without proof.

Among/Between—Among describes a relationship of more than two people or things. ("You may choose among four options.") *Between* expresses a relationship between two things ("She was caught between a rock and a hard place.")

Basic/Basically—Basic means fundamental.Its adverb form, basically is used *incorrectly* as a filler or to introduce a thought (Incorrect: "Basically, I cannot agree with your recommendation.")

Different—It's usually different *from.* Thus, a claims adjudication may be *different from* a previous case.

Few/Fewer/Less—Few means not many. (The director had few alternatives.) Fewer means a small number ("fewer people"). *Less* is comparative and means a smaller amount of something. (I had less homework last night than the night before.)

Mitigate/Militate—Mitigate means to soften or lessen. (The judge mitigated the sentence from 15 years to 5 years.) *Militate* means to weigh in favor of something. (The strong sentiment of the voters militated in favor of a tax cut.)

Principle/Principal —A *principle* is a fundamental truth or standard. (Filling jobs based upon friendship would violate the merit system principle.) *Principal* indicates main, chief or foremost. (The *principal* reason for rejecting your bid was cost.)

Emphasize / Sympathize—Emphasize means to place special value of importance on something. ("I must *emphasize* how important it is to get the report out today.") *Symphathize* means to feel compassion for another person. ("I *sympathize* with the loss of your grandmother."

Good / Well—Good is an adjective that refers to the quality of something. ("This is a *good* report.") *Well* is an adverb with a similar meaning. It is often used to refer to something done in a praiseworthy manner. ("This report was *well* done.") Don't try to impress anyone by saying "This report was done good."

Further / Farther—Further means additional or more. ("I need *further* help on this project.") *Farther* means more distant such as "Your house is *farther* away than mine."

There / Their / They're—There usually means in or toward a place. ("Let's hold the meeting over there.") *Their* is a possessive version of "they" meaning that something belongs to them. ("Their work on this task was outstanding.") *They're* means "they are" as in the sentence "They're going to meet with the division director this afternoon."

EXERCISES

1. Rewrite the following passage to create more vivid images of the problem being described:

> Anthony Robinson is consistently late in arriving at work. Repeated counseling of Robinson has not resulted in any improvement. His co-workers are complaining to me that they must do his work as well as their own. This has created a severe morale problem.

2. Make conscious word choices in the following paragraph which add to the flow and impact of your message.

> We need to (improve/upgrade/rehabilitate) our existing computer (array/system/methodology). Our (hardware/ terminal/hard disc capability) is truly (ancient/outdated/old). If we don't make a (significant/ large/ substantial) dollar investment this budget (year/cycle/ period) we will (drop/lag/fall) further and further behind. Each year we (stall/delay/procrastinate), the cost to catch up will (expand/spiral/increase).

3. Replace the formal words with informal alternatives.

A) I wish to apprise you of the progress we have made and the requirement to expedite completion of this undertaking.

B) To facilitate appeals of health benefits denials, please transmit a copy of the SF-62 to personnel immediately. While Headquarters Benefits Section is available to render advise in difficult cases, Headquarters deems it appropriate to resolve most problems in the locality in which you reside.

4. Replace the complex word groups with simpler alternatives.

Please submit your requests for holiday leave to Jean Smith by November 1. At this time, many of you will have "use or lose" leave which must be utilized by the end of the year. As of this date, I see no problem with granting leave requests. In the event of conflicts, those with the most agency seniority will receive first preference.

5. Correct the misused terms.

   A. To implement the consultant's study, the principle need will be for flexibility on your part.

   B. The review staff is composed of three work units.

   C. You will have to choose between more training, more travel or a slightly larger staff.

   D. We hope that all this new information will effect John's thinking concerning staff cuts.

Chapter Five

Add Power And Punch With Action Verbs

Chapter 5

Add Power and Punch With Action Verbs

There are several simple tricks writers can use to pack more power into letters, memos and reports. These basic techniques are common to all good writing and you don't need an advanced degree or an intensive week-long course to apply them. The four key steps to more powerful writing are:

1. Use action verbs

2. Maintain vivid images

3. Keep your word choices fresh

4. Avoid the passive voice whenever possible.

The most important of these four keys, and the easiest to master, is using action verbs. We government writers have inherited a disease from our forbears. The disease is called "nouniness." To insure that we sound authoritative, official or even stodgy, we have cultivated a love affair with nouns. Most of the words we use in daily writing have both noun and verb forms. Amazingly, we get to choose between the noun form of a word and the verb form each time we write a document. *We do have a choice.*

Consider for a moment that the ideas expressed by several people in a meeting may collide, they don't always experience a collision. Employees occasionally complain, they don't always register a complaint. Initiatives are rejected, they don't always experience a rejection. Budget cuts may destroy your plans for additional staff, they don't always suffer destruction. Scan the following list illustrating options in choosing the verb form or the noun form of some common terms.

Verb Form	Noun Form
advise	advice
break	break
caution	caution
collide	collision
connect	connection
consider	consideration
contend	contention
counsel	counseling
decide	decision
destroy	destruction
discipline	disciplinary action
grieve	grievance
impose	imposition
injure	injury
inquire	inquiry
meet	meeting
replace	replacement
sanction	sanction
yearn	yearning

After reading the list above, guess which writers tend to rivet our attention and focus our thoughts? Which writers come across as dry, stuffy and a bit boring? That's right! It's the writer who uses plenty of action verbs who communicates more effectively. It is the noun addict whose writing can be a sedative. One commentator, writing on the war in the Persian Gulf, recognized the value of action verbs:

> The despot's frightened men *walked* out of the desert to *surrender* to anyone who would *have* them. The Iraquis *kissed* the hands of their captors. After all, the despot had *trained* them in this sort of thing.
>
> Faoud Adjani
> *U.S. News and World Report*
> March 11, 1991

Notice the conscious choices made by this columnist. In three short sentences, he has used <u>five</u> action verbs (walk, surrender, have, kissed and trained). But this airy, breezy writing can be destroyed in a wink. Simply convert each of Adjani's action verbs to noun forms. Here is the product:

> The despot's frightened men took a walk out of the desert and effected their surrender to the first person they saw. Some American troops received kisses on their hands. After all, the Iraqi troops had received training in this sort of thing.

Do not think that the author has lost complete touch with reality. I recognize that routine government correspondence lacks the dramatic content and urgency of war. This means that government writers in search of some zip and zing are foiled on two fronts. First, we don't have the same fodder with which to work as do journalists. Second, those who review our work (and in government someone always reviews your work) may not have seen the light. Your boss may be comfortable with the leaden and stuffy writing we have churned out for years.

While the level of drama or intensity may not be available at work, the underlying principle still has strength and vitality. The noun addict disease continues to yield heavy, plodding documents. Here are two version of a memorandum. The first is laden with noun forms; the second rewritten to inject more action verbs:

Version A - Heavy Use of Nouns

Clearly, amendment of our travel regulations is an urgent requirement. Our hesitation in acting to institute revisions at this moment in time may have raised suspicions that we'll not complete them in a timely fashion

Version B - Action Verbs Emphasized

We have an urgent need to amend our travel regulations. If we don't act now, the Council may suspect that we'll miss the deadline altogether.

Version A - Heavy Use of Nouns

If there is a continuation of this conduct, we will be forced to undertake consideration of your termination from government employment

Version B - Action Verbs Emphasized

If you continue this conduct, we will be forced to consider terminating you from government employment.

EXERCISES

1. Rewrite the following sentences, using action verbs rather than noun forms.

(A) Solicitation of at least three bids is a requirement under our contracting rules.

(B) Upon expiration of the current fiscal year, a reevaluation of the awards budget will take place.

(C) Part of your job duties is to carry out a thorough inquiry into Mr. Belknap's sudden loss of key staff.

(D) I am forwarding two separate bills for your consideration.The first makes changes in the method of pension computation. The second permits a one-time pension transfer for eligible employees.

(E) Last year's budget cuts caused the destruction of two juvenile nutrition programs. We don't see a replacement for these lost funds in the near future.

Chapter Six

The Art Of The Passive

Chapter 6

The Art of the Passive

"Oh, and note was taken. Passively, since active verbs have an unpleasant way of betraying the actor" - *John LeCarre*

What do we mean when we speak of the active voice and the passive voice? Sentences written in the active voice usually rely on action verbs. People in active sentences *hit* baseballs, *tackle* problems and *enforce* regulations. The active voice states things in a positive, direct, or even dramatic way. The actor or decision-maker is not only identified but is often highlighted, since he or she is usually the one triggering the action.

One teacher used the following passage to illustrate the passive voice:

> This is being written so the passive voice can be explained. The analyst's memos were being revised while photocopying was being done. It was observed that talking was being carried on and attention was not being paid to needed revisions.

In the passive voice, the role and identity of the actor or decision-maker is muted or softened. The emphasis in passive sentences is upon the decision, result, or outcome rather than upon the individual taking the action. Attention is generally deflected away from decision-makers. This is because in a passive sentence, the doer of the action is no longer the subject of the sentence. The receiver, or subject of the action becomes much more critical. Note these common uses of the passive in government writing:

> It has been determined that your license application lacks merit.
>
> The claim has apparently been abandoned and will not be processed further.
>
> It appears that the evidence is insufficient to support any violation of the zoning laws.

In these examples it is less than clear just who has made these important decisions. The reader has difficulty discovering what living, breathing public servant made these findings.

Shortcomings of the Passive Voice

The passive writing style has been widely criticized. Some government agencies have even informed their employees to avoid using this writing style. The criticism is surely warranted. Too many government writers hide behind the passive as a means to shirk responsibility or avoid accountability. Since a passive writing style masks the actor and softens harsh messages, it has become an undesirable crutch for some.

Some writers employ the passive voice as a cover-up. Where a straightforward, declarative sentence might be embarrassing, public officials seek shelter in the passive. Some classic government pronouncements in the passive voice include:

> It has been determined that you do not qualify for benefits under this program.
>
> During the adjudication process, your claim has been found to be deficient.
>
> As a result of your recent letter, it was decided to initiate further inquiries.
>
> An oversupply of Model M-362 has resulted in curtailment of contracting activity.
>
> Questions have been raised concerning your suitability for continued employment.

The passive voice not only compromises clear and direct communication with your audience, it requires more words to say the same thing:

Active Voice

> The Division Manager cancelled the training conference. [7 words]

Passive Voice

> The training conference was cancelled by the Division Manager. [9 words]

Active Voice

In order to sustain disciplinary action against the employee, be sure to apply the principles of progressive discipline. [17 words]

Passive Voice

If your discipline of the employee is to be sustained, it must be remembered that principles of progressive discipline are to be applied. [23 words]

Effective Use of the Passive Voice

There are certainly occasions where a passive writing style can be used to your advantage. But use caution! When a government writer lapses into the passive voice, readers go on the defensive. As the author of your letter or memo, you have unconsciously signaled that you are hedging or trying to mask people or events. A second risk with this type of writing is that it weighs down your sentences by using unnecessary words.

Nevertheless, the passive voice can be a useful tool for the government writer. Here are several situations where the passive can help make your communication more effective:

Placing The Actor's Identity At The End Of A Sentence Adds Dramatic Effect

It was concluded that these vital records had been destroyed by the commissioner.

Where The Thing Being Done Is Of Vital Importance, But The Person Doing It Is Not.

During the investigation, it was shown that the employee had lied on his initial application for employment. Even the college degree was a fabrication. These facts, uncovered by the Inspector General, proved to be vital.

When You Want To Protect The Identity Of The Decision-maker

I regret to inform you that further review of your case has been denied.

When The Active Voice Simply Sounds Better

The procurement officer reviewed the bids. The Director of Acquisition and Logistics studied the initial technical requirements. Finally, they agreed that the document had been misread by both of them.

You Wish to Criticize with Finesse

It seems that this situation could have been better handled by the review staff.

Avoiding Repetitive His / her Or He / she

Active

A bidder must submit his/her proposal with the contracting office. He/she must state his/her technical qualifications along with a fixed price bid.

Passive

A fixed price contract bid must be submitted to the contracting office by May 5. A statement of technical qualifications must accompany each proposal.

EXERCISES

1. Change the following passive sentences to the active voice.

A. It has been determined that further interviews of applicants are unnecessary. A decision has been made to select from among the current pool of candidates.

B. In all cases where new regulations were implemented, a second opportunity for public response was thought appropriate.

C. The defects were initially hidden and became apparent only after in-depth testing of the samples.

D. No action has been taken. No timely response has been received. Questions have arisen concerning your continued interest in this project.

2. Change the following active sentences to the passive voice.

A. I find your work unacceptable. You've sent me shoddy, incomplete calculations. I cannot rely on you to complete a job without constant prodding.

B. When the vice-president accepted a cash bribe, the nation was shocked and outraged.

C. I am denying your appeal. You failed to bring me any new evidence that your company should have been selected for the public works contract. With regret, I am closing your case file.

Chapter Seven

Dealing With Gender And Sexism

Chapter 7

Dealing with Gender and Sexism

In my own field of specialization—employment law—I see many documents containing language like this:

> When the masculine gender is used in this agreement it shall include the feminine gender as well.

Woman are tired of that and writers in government should not use it. The time has come to strike sexist language and sexual stereotypes from our documents.

An effective writer uses sex-neutral word choices where it is natural to do so—staffing requirements instead of manpower requirements—reasonable people instead of reasonable men. On the other hand, don't dredge up awkward terms like "waitpersons" to refer to restaurant servers. Nor does your agency's public ombudsman have to be converted into an ombudsperson.

Be consistent and accord similar status and rank when referring to male/female pairs. Director and Mrs. Janko, not Director Janko and Peggy; husbands and wives, not men and wives. Try the plural instead of the singular (all of our employees believe they have contributed to our success, not each employee believes *he* has contributed to our success.)

You also have the option of alternating the feminine and masculine pronoun. If *he* refers to branch chiefs in one paragraph, try using *she* to refer to chemists in another paragraph. This is preferable to the he/she solution which is an awkward one.

> A personnel intern must complete a 90 day rotation in each of three specialties—recruitment, classification and employee relations. He/she will be given an opportunity to select a permanent assignment after he/she has completed all three phases of the rotation.

The he/she awkwardness can be overcome by using plurals which are sex-neutral.

> Personnel interns must complete a 90 day rotation in each of three specialties—recruitment, classification and employee relations. They will be given an opportunity to select a permanent assignment after they have completed all three phases of the rotation.

Deleting the overworked masculine and feminine pronouns (his/her) is another approach worth considering:

> A property owner may obtain a review of her tax assessment by filing an appeal of her initial tax bill for 1992.

> A property owner may obtain review of an initial tax assessment by appealing the initial 1991 tax bill.

EXERCISES

1. Remove the sexist or gender-specific references from these paragraphs and rewrite.

A. A driver must complete his or her automobile log at the end of each trip. He/she must include the purpose of the trip, the distance traveled and the time of return.

B. Regional Director Ames and his wife Peggy attended the awards ceremony in Chicago. Other key members of the management team attended with their wives.

C. An effective secretary must ensure that her correspondence is organized and that she has updated all her computer files.

D. Each and every analyst must think for herself.

E. A contractor's resume should accurately reflect his technical qualifications.

Chapter Eight

Summary

Summary

The ability to write clearly and effectively continues to be a critical skill for government professionals. In recent years we've seen dramatic changes in the public service. These changes have impacted both what we do and how we do it. The nature of the services demanded by the public and the way in which we deliver those services is not the same as it was ten years ago. Like most enterprises in the United States, government service has not been immune from the "high-tech" revolution. There will soon be a personal computer on the desk of virtually every civil servant. New economic realities have made terms like "budget cuts", "downsizing" and "staffing shortage" a part of our daily work vocabulary.

While most aspects of government service have seen evolutionary or even revolutionary changes, the need for clear written communications remains constant. From entry level positions to senior executive, from clerk-typist to Division Chief, we continue to be judged and evaluated through our written products. Strong writers are always in demand. They will continue to be a valuable commodity.

Some government careerists have worked their way to the top of the heap through sound writing skills. More and more vacancy announcements request a writing sample. Annual appraisals require supervisors to assess the writing skills of subordinates.

Written communication is one constant in our jobs. Skills or deficiencies in this area can make or break a career. Managers complain loudly when they receive poorly written drafts. They heave a sigh of relieve when a subordinate's written assignment is letter perfect. This book was written because the quality of your writing as a government professional directly impacts your personal career aspirations. Producing a top quality report, letter or memorandum is a demanding task. Surely, no single course or book can cure every writing ill or remedy every flaw in style. Better writing is decidedly a process, not a single isolated event or occurrence.

Applying the principles in this book is one important step in the *process* of better writing. As we have tried to point out in these pages, there is much to be hopeful about. Some fundamental improvements may flow from thinking through our writing task before we put pen to paper. For example, a sound plan of attack and a resolve to meet the reader's needs are both positive steps in this direction. We can make substantial strides by merely staying focused on three objectives:

1. Making it easy for the writer to digest information

2. Providing insight into the problem or issue being discussed

3. Helping the reader make sound and supportable decisions

To succeed in this sacred writing mission, few of us start from ground zero. There is no need to completely revamp our approach to writing. Rather, a few simple and straightforward steps can add polish, persuasion and impact to our existing style. Minor adjustments such as trimming the fat from a sentence, adding an action verb or fine-tuning a word choice can all move us steadily along the path to superior writing.

We hope that this book will help you in your quest for writing excellence.

Answer Key

ANSWER KEY

The following answers reflect *one possible* answer to the problems posed. You may develop a better version.

Chapter 1

1. It was before dawn when Sue arrived at work. She entered her dark office, flipped on the light switch and turned on her computer. Glancing across the hall, Sue was shocked to see John Hall silently slumped in his chair.

2. Working for the Federal Government is both exciting and challenging. You will have the chance to move ahead. We send employees to both on-site and off-site training. Our pay and benefits package is second to none.

3. On the morning of November 9, Channel 7 predicted a substantial snow storm. The following day, a snow storm did hit the area, paralyzing traffic. In fact, the storm caused many roads to become impassable. Many employees could not get into work on November 10. Early on the morning of November 11, employees were told that absences the previous day would be excused.

Version A

> Bob Lofgren should be issued a letter of reprimand for his irresponsible action last week. Lofgren alone is responsible for monitoring all federal grant applications. His failure to meet the required deadline is inexcusable. By

failing to perform his duties, he caused the agency a loss of $50,000. According to our disciplinary handbook, section 202.04, a letter of reprimand is called for.

Version B

Bob Lofgren made a mistake last week when the agency missed the filing deadline on a single grant application for a storm sewer project. In his previous 5 years on the job, Lofgren has never missed a single deadline of this kind. Bob admits his error. The facts will show that his oldest son was hospitalized during the week in question and that he was under extreme pressure at home. It is only fair and equitable to apply Disciplinary Handbook Rule 204 (b) in this case. Bob's spotless work record is clear evidence that this will never happen again.

5. Government employees cannot accept anything of value from a contractor who is now doing, or may in the future, do business with his agency.

Each government pay grade has within it a range of steps. For example a grade 12 employee begins at step one and may progress through step 10.

So long as performance is satisfactory, an employee will advance one step each year. However, once the employee reaches step 10, he or she is "maxed out" and can receive no further step increase.

It doesn't appear that our staffing needs for next fiscal year will be met. Our only hope is to convince the cabinet secretary to allocate more dollars.

We will no longer honor speaking requests from environmental groups. These groups repeatedly attacked agency positions and have not allowed us a fair chance to respond. Our time and resources are not well spent on such public appearances.

Chapter 2

1. You are entitled to receive quality service with no errors. Everyone benefits when you receive better service.

The documents will be available any time after 1 p.m. on Friday, October 18. We can provide photocopies upon request.

2. Recommendations for cash awards must be received by December 1. Recommendations must be endorsed by both the Section Chief and the Division Manager.

I have attached a copy of standard form SF-23. Keep this form in mind when ordering office supplies, or purchasing new office equipment.

3. A. There are a number of alternative approaches we should look at.

   B. There are several ways we might improve next year's program.

Chapter 3

1. Replace the lengthy word groups with simpler choices.

A. Our investigation shows that the Branch Chief acted under current procedures in handling the May 23 incident.

B. This responds to your inquiry about your step increase.

2. Tighten up each passage by maximizing **brick** words and reducing the number of mortar words.

A. Regulations are often too poorly written for taxpayers to understand.

B. Williams' explanation did not seem logical.

C. Employees are not allowed to accept gifts or meals from contractors where they may play a role in contractor selection.

D. You may only park in a reserved or handicapped space if you have the proper sticker for these spaces.

Version 1

All taxpayers are reminded that appeals of property tax assessment must be filed by October 1. Any appeal postmarked after that date will not be processed. If you need a tax appeal form telephone 555-1212 or you can send a self-addressed envelope. You can expect action on your appeal within 60 days of filing.

Version 2

This year's appeal deadline of October 1 will be strictly enforced. Do not take action on any appeal postmarked after that date. Each reviewer is expected to comply with a 60 day turnaround. We are trying to get more overtime funds to help you clear any case backlog.

Version 3

This year, the Tax Appeal Division will be strictly enforcing the October 1 filing deadline. Because of recent tax hikes, we expect a record number of appeals this year. Our staff has been given strict deadlines within which to complete reviews. We will need a supplemental appropriation to assure that time targets are met and to assure proper taxpayer service.

CHAPTER 4

1. Rewrite the following passage to create more vivid images of the problem being described.

> Anthony Robinson arrives at work late day after day. Despite counseling time and again, his habits have not changed at all. His coworkers are angry and frustrated because Robinson's absences have increased their work load. Morale is at an all time low.

2. Make conscious word choices to add to the flow and impact of your message.

> We need to *upgrade* our existing computer *system*. Our *hardware* is truly *outdated*. If we don't make a *significant* dollar investment this budget *cycle*, we will *fall* further and further behind. Each year we *delay*, the cost to catch up will *increase*.

3. Replace the formal words with informal alternatives.

> A. I want to update you about the progress we've made and the need to speed up completion of this project.
>
> B. Health benefits denials can be handled with ease if you will send along a copy of SF-62 to personnel. Headquarters Benefits Section is there to help out with the really tough cases. You should, however, be able to solve most problems in the area in which you live.

4. Replace the complex word groups with simpler alternatives.

Please submit your requests for holiday leave to Jean Smith by November 1. Many of you now have "use or lose" leave which must be used by the end of the year. Right now, I see no problem granting leave requests. If conflicts do arise, those with the most agency seniority will receive first preferences.

5. Correct the misused terms.

A. *principal* need

B. *comprised* of

C. choose *among*

D. will *affect* John's thinking.

Chapter 5

Rewrite the following sentences, using action verbs rather than noun forms.

A. It's required that you solicit at least three bids under our regulations.

B. After the fiscal year ends, we will reevaluate the awards budget.

C. As part of your job, you should inquire why Mr. Belknap has lost so many key staff members.

D. I am forwarding two separate bills for you to consider. The first version changes the formula for computing pensions. The second version actually transfers employees' funds on a one-time basis.

E. Last year's budget cuts totally destroyed two programs. We don't see any way to replace these funds in the near future.

Chapter 6

1. Change the following passive sentences to the active voice.

A. I decided that it is not necessary to interview any more applicants. We decided to select someone from our current candidate pool.

B. It's appropriate to give the public a second opportunity for comment when we implement new rules.

C. After in-depth testing, many of the product's defects surfaced.

D. I question whether you're really still interested in this project. You've done nothing and you haven't submitted any response.

2. Change the following active sentences to the passive voice.

A. It has been concluded that your work is no longer acceptable. The calculations submitted were shoddy and incomplete. You cannot be relied upon to complete a job without being prodded.

B. Acceptance of a bribe by the vice-president caused shock and outrage throughout the nation.

C. Your appeal has been denied. No new evidence was submitted explaining why you should have been selected. Please be advised that the case file in this matter has been closed.

Chapter 7

Remove the sexist or gender-specific references from these paragraphs and rewrite.

A. Drivers must complete their automobile logs at the end of each trip. The driver's entry must include the purpose of the trip, the distance traveled and the time of return.

B. Director and Mrs. Ames attended the awards ceremony in Chicago. Other key members of the management team attended with their spouses.

C. To be effective, a secretary must insure that all correspondence is organized and all computer files are updated.

D. Each and every analyst must think for him or herself.

E. The resumes of contractors should reflect their technical background.

Training Seminars Available from FPMI

The Federal Personnel Management Institute, Inc. specializes in training seminars for Federal managers and supervisors. These seminars can be conducted at your worksite at a per person rate that is substantially less than open enrollment seminars.

The instructors for FPMI seminars have all had practical experience with the Federal Government and know problems Federal supervisors face and how to deal effective with those problems.

Some of the seminar-workshops available include:

- "Managing Unionized Employees Effectively"
- "Developing Effective Performance Standards"
- "Managing Problem Employees"
- "Basic Labor Relations Workshop"
- "Negotiations Workshop"
- "Managing Labor Relations Conflict"
- "Preventing Sexual Harassment"
- "Managing Cultural Diversity"
- "Effective EEO Leadership"
- "Legal Writing for Non-Lawyers
- "Handling ULP Disputes"
- "Conducting Fact-Finding and Administrative Investigations"
- "Petitions, Elections and Bargaining Unit Exclusions"

For more training information, call (205) 539-1850 or fax (205) 539-0911